CHAMELEONS

by Imogen Kingsley

AMICUS | AMICUS INK

Amicus High Interest and Amicus Ink are imprints of Amicus
P.O. Box 1329, Mankato, MN 56002
www.amicuspublishing.us

Library of Congress Cataloging-in-Publication Data
Names: Kingsley, Imogen, author.
Title: Chameleons / by Imogen Kingsley.
Description: Mankato, Minnesota : Amicus/Amicus Ink, [2019] | Series: Lizards in the wild | Audience: K to Grade 3. | Includes index.
Identifiers: LCCN 2018002372 (print) | LCCN 2018006675 (ebook) | ISBN 9781681515939 (pdf) | ISBN 9781681515557 (library binding) | ISBN 9781681523934 (paperback)
Subjects: LCSH: Chameleons--Juvenile literature.
Classification: LCC QL666.L23 (ebook) | LCC QL666.L23 K49 2019 (print) | DDC 597.95/6--dc23
LC record available at https://lccn.loc.gov/2018002372

Photo Credits: Shutterstock/Kuttelvaserova Stuchelova cover, 2, 22, Shulevskyy Volodymyr 5, Pierre-Yves Babelon 6, CeriDJones 10–11, Igor Grochev 13, Svoboda Pavel 16–17; Getty/Nigel Pavitt 9, Jack Milchanowski 14, Suzanne L Collins 20–21; Alamy/David Keith Jones 18

Editor: Mary Ellen Klukow
Designer: Peggie Carley & Ciara Beitlich
Photo Researcher: Holly Young

Printed in China

HC 10 9 8 7 6 5 4 3 2 1
PB 10 9 8 7 6 5 4 3 2 1

TABLE OF CONTENTS

MANY KINDS

Chameleons are lizards. Like all lizards, they are **cold-blooded**. There are many kinds. Some are as small as your toe. Some are as big as a cat. A few have horns.

Check This Out
Jackson's chameleons have horns. They use them to fight.

WHERE THEY LIVE

Most chameleons live in Africa.

Some live in the rainforest.

Others are found in the desert.

Some even live in the mountains.

The island of **Madagascar** is

home to over 75 kinds.

Check This Out

Many of these lizards are endangered. They
lose their homes when people cut down trees.

MANY COLORS

Chameleons can change colors. They change to warm up or cool down. They can change to show their mood. Bright colors mean "stay away from me!"

LAYERS OF SKIN

A chameleon has four layers of skin. The skin is made of **cells**. Some cells carry color. Some are **transparent**. To change color, a lizard moves its cells to reflect the light differently.

HANDY FEET

A chameleon is a good climber.
It can climb straight up a branch.
Its feet have long toes. They
hold on to branches when the
lizard hunts.

GOOGLY EYES

Look at those eyes! They can move separately. This helps the chameleon see all around. Chameleons use their eyes to hunt.

A FAST TONGUE

Look! A grasshopper! The lizard opens her mouth. Her tongue zips out. It is sticky. It is long. It is fast. She grabs the bug. Yum!

A HELPFUL TAIL

Look! A chameleon's tail can curl up tight. It can also grab branches. It holds on. His tail helps the chameleon keep his balance.

Check This Out
Unlike other lizards, if a chameleon's tail breaks off, it cannot grow a new one.

20

HATCHLINGS

Baby chameleons hatch from their eggs. Mom is not there. That's okay. The **hatchlings** can walk. They can hunt. They can take care of themselves.

A LOOK AT
A CHAMELEON

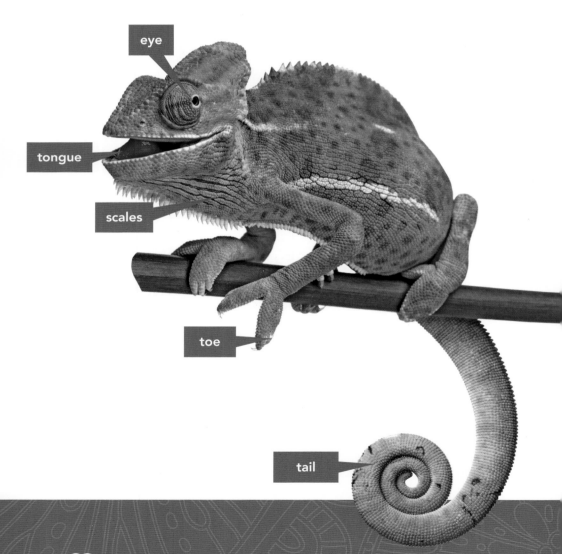

eye

tongue

scales

toe

tail

WORDS TO KNOW

cell The smallest unit of life; your body is made up of different kinds of cells.

cold-blooded When an animal's body temperature changes to be the same as the temperature of its surroundings.

endangered In danger of becoming extinct.

hatchling A young chameleon.

Madagascar An African island nation rich in animal life.

transparent Clear like glass; you can easily see through it.

LEARN MORE

Books

Bodden, Valerie. *Chameleons*. Mankato, Minn.: Creative Education, 2016.

Kenney, Karen Latchana. *Super Chameleons*. Minneapolis: Jump! Inc., 2018.

Websites

DK Find Out!
https://www.dkfindout.com/us/animals-and-nature/reptiles/chameleons/

National Geographic
http://kids.nationalgeographic.com/animals/chameleon/

San Diego Zoo
http://animals.sandiegozoo.org/animals/chameleon

INDEX